MAJOR DISASTERS

FUKUSHIMA

BY ROBERT LEROSE

WWW.APEXEDITIONS.COM

Copyright © 2024 by Apex Editions, Mendota Heights, MN 55120. All rights reserved. No part of this book may be reproduced or utilized in any form or by any means without written permission from the publisher.

Apex is distributed by North Star Editions:
sales@northstareditions.com | 888-417-0195

Produced for Apex by Red Line Editorial.

Photographs ©: Hiro Komae/AP Images, cover; Shutterstock Images, 1, 8, 10–11, 14–15, 18, 20–21, 24–25; Hidenori Nagai/The Yomiuri Shimbun/AP Images, 4–5; Kyodo News/AP Images, 6–7; Yasushi Nagao/The Yomiuri Shimbun/AP Images, 12–13; Kaname Yoneyama/The Yomiuri Shimbun/AP Images, 16–17; Wally Santana/AP Images, 19, 29; Masanori Genko/The Yomiuri Shimbun/AP Images, 22–23; Kentaro Tominaga/The Yomiuri Shimbun/AP Images, 26–27

Library of Congress Control Number: 2023910178

ISBN
978-1-63738-757-3 (hardcover)
978-1-63738-800-6 (paperback)
978-1-63738-883-9 (ebook pdf)
978-1-63738-843-3 (hosted ebook)

Printed in the United States of America
Mankato, MN
012024

NOTE TO PARENTS AND EDUCATORS
Apex books are designed to build literacy skills in striving readers. Exciting, high-interest content attracts and holds readers' attention. The text is carefully leveled to allow students to achieve success quickly. Additional features, such as bolded glossary words for difficult terms, help build comprehension.

CHAPTER 1
DANGEROUS WAVES 4

CHAPTER 2
HOW IT HAPPENED 10

CHAPTER 3
DAMAGE 16

CHAPTER 4
SLOW RECOVERY 22

COMPREHENSION QUESTIONS • 28
GLOSSARY • 30
TO LEARN MORE • 31
ABOUT THE AUTHOR • 31
INDEX • 32

CHAPTER 1

DANGEROUS WAVES

It is March 11, 2011. People walk along the beach in Okuma, Japan. But deep under the ocean, an earthquake shakes the ground.

Okuma is one of several towns near the Fukushima nuclear power plant.

The tsunami flooded many areas along Japan's coast.

Giant waves form out in the ocean. Soon, a tsunami is racing toward Japan's coast. Deep, fast water crashes over the land.

FAST FACT

One of the waves that hit Japan was 33 feet (10 m) high.

7

The water floods streets and destroys buildings. A nuclear power plant near Okuma is also damaged. It begins sending out dangerous **radiation**.

EXPLOSION AT FUKUSHIMA

The Fukushima power plant used nuclear **reactors**. Hot **cores** in the reactors made electricity. After the tsunami, three of these cores exploded.

 A tsunami's waves are powerful enough to fling large boats.

CHAPTER 2

HOW IT HAPPENED

The earthquake was caused by shifting **plates** under the Pacific Ocean. Their movement made waves at the top of the water.

The earthquake near Fukushima was very strong. It caused damage throughout Japan.

The waves started small. But they began traveling toward Japan. As they moved, they grew bigger and faster.

FAST FACT
At one point, the tsunami was moving nearly 500 miles per hour (800 km/h).

Some tsunami waves began to swirl as they neared Japan's coast.

13

Within about 20 minutes, the waves reached land. They caused massive flooding. Many places lost power. The Fukushima power plant was one of them.

Floodwater in some areas was more than 13 feet (4 m) deep.

Too Hot

The power plant's cooling system used electricity. Without power, it stopped working. Three cores got superhot. They melted holes through the floor. Radiation leaked into the air.

CHAPTER 3

DAMAGE

The tsunami destroyed more than 380,000 buildings throughout Japan. Around 20,000 people were killed or went missing.

16

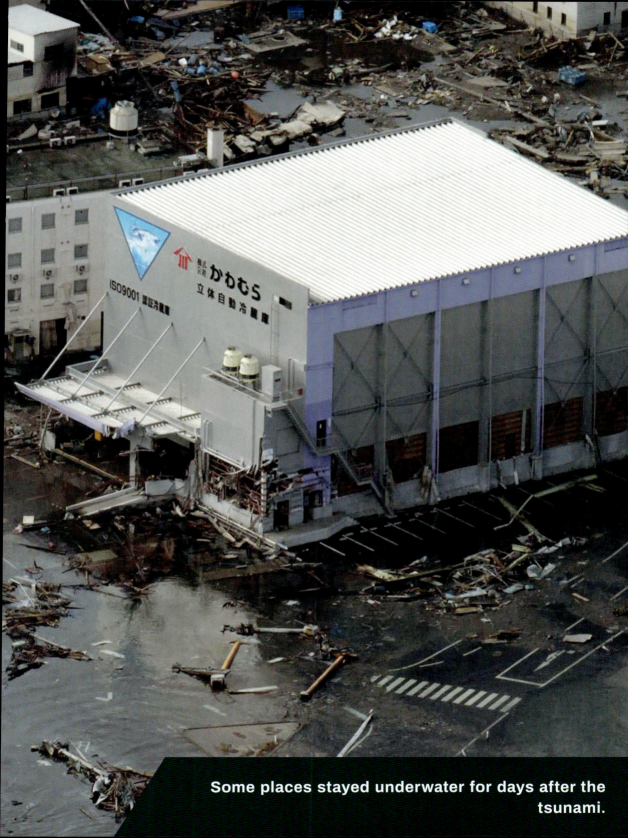

Some places stayed underwater for days after the tsunami.

FAST FACT The power plant kept releasing radiation for six days after the tsunami.

Workers checked people's bodies for radiation. Too much radiation can make people very sick.

The damaged power plant spilled radiation into the air and the ocean. The radiation got into people's food and water. Both became unsafe.

◀ Radiation got into soil near the power plant. Workers collected this soil in bags.

Metal gates blocked off areas near the power plant that were unsafe to enter.

To keep people safe, the area near the plant was **evacuated**. No one could go within 12.5 miles (20 km) of it. Thousands of people had to leave their homes.

COOLING DOWN

Workers tried to cool the reactors. Helicopters flew over the plant and dropped water on it. Workers also shot water from cannons. Still, it took several months for the reactors to cool back down.

CHAPTER 4

SLOW RECOVERY

Japan and other countries worked to help the area recover. They sent food and other supplies. They also helped clean up **debris**.

Workers checked damaged areas for survivors.

Workers fixed or replaced highways, railroads, and buildings. They also built a **seawall**. It would help protect the area from future tsunamis.

WARNING SYSTEMS

Warning systems are a key part of preparing for tsunamis. **Seismic** stations around the world sense earthquakes. They warn places a tsunami might hit. That gives people time to get ready.

Several towns along Japan's coast added seawalls. These walls help block tsunami waves.

Cleanup work near the power plant continued for more than 10 years. Gradually, radiation levels lowered. People slowly began returning to the area.

FAST FACT
By 2022, almost all areas were declared safe for people to start going back to.

COMPREHENSION QUESTIONS

Write your answers on a separate piece of paper.

1. Write a few sentences describing how the Fukushima power plant was damaged.

2. Do you think nuclear power plants are too dangerous? Why or why not?

3. How far away from the power plant did people have to stay?
   - **A.** 33 feet (10 m)
   - **B.** 12.5 miles (20 km)
   - **C.** 100 miles (161 km)

4. Which event happened first?
   - **A.** the earthquake under the ocean
   - **B.** the tsunami that hit the coast
   - **C.** the explosion at the power plant

5. What does **recover** mean in this book?

*Japan and other countries worked to help the area **recover**. They sent food and other supplies.*

    A. fall apart
    B. make money
    C. get better

6. What does **gradually** mean in this book?

*Cleanup work near the power plant continued for more than 10 years. **Gradually**, radiation levels lowered.*

    A. right away
    B. in just a short time
    C. slowly over time

Answer key on page 32.

29

GLOSSARY

cores
The parts of nuclear reactors that contain the fuel and produce the energy.

debris
Pieces of something that broke or fell apart.

evacuated
Moved people away from a dangerous place.

plates
Huge pieces of Earth's crust that move and turn.

radiation
Tiny particles sent out by a nuclear reaction.

reactors
Devices used to make and control nuclear reactions that produce power.

seawall
A wall built on a coast to protect the land from ocean waves.

seismic
Related to earthquakes or other movements of Earth's crust.

BOOKS

Harkrader, Lisa. *Nuclear Power*. Parker, CO: The Child's World, 2023.

MacCarald, Clara. *Investigating Nuclear Pollution*. Mankato, MN: The Child's World, 2023.

Rathburn, Betsy. *Tsunamis*. Minneapolis: Bellwether Media, 2020.

ONLINE RESOURCES

Visit **www.apexeditions.com** to find links and resources related to this title.

ABOUT THE AUTHOR

Robert Lerose was going to school in New York when a nuclear disaster happened in Pennsylvania in 1979. He survived Hurricane Gloria in 1985 and Superstorm Sandy in 2012. He likes writing about major disasters better than living through them.

INDEX

C
cores, 9, 15

E
earthquake, 4, 10, 25
electricity, 9, 15
evacuating, 21

F
flooding, 9, 14

O
Okuma, Japan, 4, 9

P
Pacific Ocean, 10
power plant, 9, 14–15, 18–19, 21, 27

R
radiation, 9, 15, 18–19, 27
reactors, 9, 21

S
seawall, 24

T
tsunami, 6, 9, 12, 16, 18, 24–25

W
warning systems, 25
waves, 6–7, 10, 12

ANSWER KEY:
1. Answers will vary; 2. Answers will vary; 3. B; 4. A; 5. C; 6. C